DROWNING KITTENS

and

ROAD GODS

Drowning Kittens and Road Gods

POETRY BY *Paul Angelosanto*

PHOTOGRAPHY AND ARTWORK BY
Gregory Damien Grinnell,
T.G. Yearwood, AND *David Stickney*

A Vampire Pigeons Production 1997

Cover image by David Stickney and Gregory Damien Grinnell.
Model: Laura Clifford

ISBN 0-9662086-0-9
Library of Congress catalog no. 97-95293

Contact the author online at
www.astroal.com

for

Mary Elizabeth Davenport Angelosanto

1929—1995

the most gorgeous of all creatures

Contents

Foreword   9

Drowning Kittens   13

Fractures   16

A Lost Romantic on Jack's Highways and Byways   18

From The Jungle   22

The Zen of Pez   24

Out In The Open   27

Al's Adventures In Space   29

The Undead Lover   32

Icon   34

If It Wasn't For Paranoia I Wouldn't Have Any Friends   37

Derelict   39

A Blade of Grass   45

Varney the Vampire and I   50

Road Gods   59

Foreword

Let me do your thinking for you. Celebrities of nothing. Trial by mass media over-saturation. Childproof the world. A collection of mantras for our times. These are the ways we seem to live now and in this moment of now that is the way I write. These are poems of now. Yet the past is a now too. We are forever retro, so that is here as well.

These are separate thoughts, feelings, and stories of the bright and the bleak. They are the weight of a bag full of live kittens that will either be carried to a glittering new home or thrown into a river. They are yin and yang, capsulated, defined, and rhymed.

"Road Gods" is an epic poem. A poetic tale of blood, love, and modern-day deities. If it is truly about anything, it is about the empty morass of nothing that people find themselves unable to escape. I think it travels along well with the shorter poems.

Before we proceed, I would like to thank everyone who helped out with my previous effort, *The Season of Passage,* and this book. It has meant more to me than I can express. Thanks to my musical compatriots, Al Finn and Bob Ross for playing alongside me at so many readings. Thanks are also due to T.G., David, and Greg for making this happen. I would particularly like to thank Chris Hinckley, the man who first believed in Astro Al and allowed the original version of "Al's Adventures in Space" to see its first printing in the pages of *Instant Magazine.* I would also especially like to thank my mother for telling me about the cats.

Paul Angelosanto
Stoneham, Massachusetts
1997

Drowning
Kittens

Drowning Kittens

Slaying stray ghosts
with words
is all I can do
by writing about
this pond
this dark collection
of water
that eagerly
accepted
the tied sack
full of kittens
who had yet
to even see
the horror of
this world
they had been borne
into
the offspring of cats
who knew not how
empty their masters were

Sliced above
the navel
in a trash bag
in a garbage crypt
Karina Holmer
was strangled
drowned in the

morass of the
land she thought
she loved

Burying a memory
without leaving
a headstone
is all I hope to
do
by scribbling about
this pond of the expired
I don't want to fathom
its depths
and understand
the cruelty
of the drowning kittens

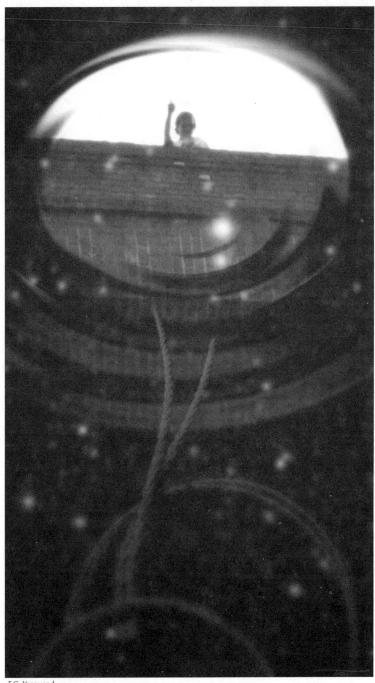

T.G. Yearwood

Fractures

Can't you see we're
growing apart
in the books we read
in the films we see
in the plays ...
we pretend to be

You were chasing snowflakes on Summer lawns
I was sweating over empty pages
growing numbers of separate dawns

Obsessions lead to possessions
changes too small to see
too many times we disagree

The click of your heels
as you walk away
striking memories of Ferris wheels

Snow-blind you stumble on
while I sit alone
with pages
no longer so empty

David Stickney

A Lost Romantic on Jack's Highways and Byways

A raven came to me a-cawing

and a-yakking

"Though thy crest be shorn and shaven, thou," I said,

"art sure no craven."

he looked at me and said,

"Right on Daddy-O. I'm gonna take you to a magic haven."

So we blasted down RTE 66

screamin' all the way

Iron City beer cans rolling empty behind us like lost souls

tied to a newlywed's bumper

Days flew by and dreams liquefied as I injected it all into my veins

finally in a haze I turned to the raven

I gazed at his dripping darkness 'til I scarcely more than

    muttered,

"Other friends have flown before."

He said, "Man, you're one weird mammajamma. Hang a left here.

I don't want to end up in Baltimore."

We passed some hitchhiker. His name was Edgar according to his

cardboard sign.

I'm glad we didn't pick him up. He stank of cheap wine.

So we drove on through states both mental and national that had

no names we blazed on burning up some new superhighways

passed some weird intersection, think it was called Internet.

We ripped through crawling neon reflections and rejections

we were new pioneers

Asphalt astronomers

Still I felt my heart dangling from its place on my sleeve

Kinda like the fuzzy dice a-danglin' from

the mirror that the raven, that mad

---

maven, liked so much

he belched

"Wretch," I cried, "Thy God hath lent thee—by these angels he

hath sent thee."

"Dig," said the raven, "When are you gonna get hep, cat?"

So we sojourned onwards

blew past another hitchhiker who

was muttering about some gold mine

with snakes and newts crawling all about him. I believe his name

was Mr. Mojo

lost him in a backwash haze of

ozone chewin' exhaust

he was a creepy, seepy, leapy dude

as he yelled, "I can do anything!"

"Let's see you do a handspring!" yelled the raven

over his obsidian wing

So we tore on and the road wore on

down past mutant gas stations

cheap cheeze burgers

black velvet Elvis

mad tourist creations, crazy Disney machinations, bewildering

glimmering fruitations, slithering scissoring exclamations,

up past chia lawns

fallen prawns, chewed fax cables, overturned overripe tables,

upscale ethernet cables, broken Clark Gables, girls too tawn,

chairs half sawn, suburban dawns, and many

infinities of yawns

Finally

everything came into a focus

There's a signpost up ahead

There was a vague person taking

shape from the splinters of previous

travelers ahead

The raven's feathers ruffled

with flatulence

"Take thy beak from out of my heart,

and take thy form from off my door."

He looked at me

and the me to be

taking form

"I'm splitsville."

and with that he took wing

to some distant Plutonian shore

I sighed and croaked, "Nevermore."

T.G. Yearwood

From The Jungle

She came unto me
like a deep image
from a soft dream
of a glorious Eden

She was adorned in
the finest silks and satins

She had a perfume
like the smell after
a quiet rain in a dark
secret place in a mystic
jungle

She had eyes that
held the secrets of
the magical caverns
that create the
great vault of night

She had love
like the roar of the ocean
heard on a moon starved
sunless beach

David Stickney

The Zen of Pez

Purity of sugar
in pellet form

New Orleans jazz
melted in my ears
as I replayed images
of a fractured romance

Her hand throwing down the ace of spades
the mellow reflection of the sunset above the
everglades
her slick pair of shades
pretty hotel ballroom serenades

Blowing smoke in Amsterdam
jumping into the pit for a slam
setting a fire in Las Vegas
her weaving spells over me like a magus

I take another hit
from my Tweety Bird dispenser
remembering the lines of lips
when she said,
"We'll always have the Zen of Pez."

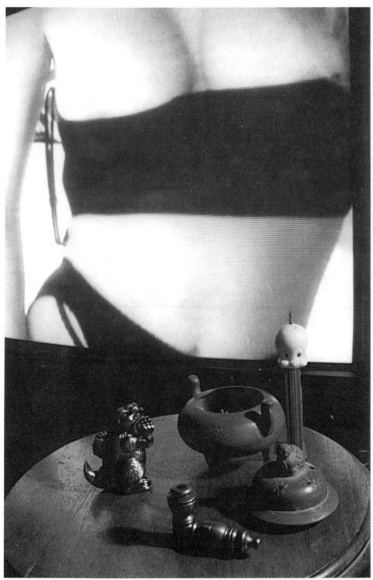

David Stickney

Gregory Damien Grinnell

Out In The Open

Worlds
are only fragmented pictures
within pictured worlds
and sterile
words
Framing angels
with her petty hands
consigned to topographic millenniums
of austere immaculation
Under the geographical vortex
of multiverses and sentinels of
stellar charts
she moves like a
dry phoenix
Folding creases
spindling and mutilating
a corner of infinity
a skin cell flakes
from her
Extinct maps
and falling
above a fabricated
forest
just in the way she stands
Words are only
charts and maps
for emotions
astrology for
the damned

Bending light
around a corner
transmogrifying
distance and serenity
in her yesterday of
purity
The trigonometry
of jackals and hyenas
consuming stale
vermin under
an unknown sun
Worlds are only
captured words
within spheres
within hemispheres
within her open
words

"Bitter sharks are dying off the shores of Venus," said the drunken spaceman

The Martian lifted his head feebly from the bar both antennas dangling like panty hose on a clothes line

"What's that you say? Another round? All right, this one's on me, chimp child," the Martian muttered

The twelve armed bartender quickly fixed their drinks

"I wish you wouldn't call me that," the spaceman said "You know I prefer Astro Al."

"Yeah, whatever," the emerald hued Martian slurred

He gulped down what must have been his fifteenth Vulcan Nerve Pinch

"So what was that you were spouting about sharks?" the Martian asked as his gangly antennas twitched in horror at the fresh intake of alcohol

"I was just thinking aloud," said Astro Al (or the spaceman if you prefer) "It's really sad about those sharks."

"What sharks?" the Martian asked as both his eyes filmed over with a fermented fog

"The sharks that never make it to Venus," said Astro Al who just decided he preferred to be called Asteroid Al but didn't want to discuss it at this juncture

"You see Venus has all these big zoos. They have animals from all over the galaxy in 'em. But they don't have any sharks. No sharks at all," Asteroid Al said

"Yeah, where did I park the star cruiser?" the Martian asked as he swayed on the barstool and one antenna chased the other around his head

Asteroid Al, who knew that he used to be called Aerodynamic Al behind his back when he was a pilot on Earth, said, "See, Venus tries to get sharks in their aquariums but they never survive the trip through space. For some reason they always die before they get there. And you know someone on Venus is always trying to bring them there and it never works. So I was just thinking that each shark must be pretty depressed that it isn't the first one to survive the trip."

"Yeah, that's a good one," the Martian said as he ordered another drink "Did I ever tell you the one about the three legged Plutonian and the human Rabbi?" the Martian asked

As the Martian began to mutter his joke (which Al was having trouble concentrating on due to the fact that he had just drunk what might have been his seventh I'm A Drunk Not A Doctor Daiquiri) Asteroid Al decided he should change his nick-name back to Astro Al due to the fact that he didn't want to change his space stationary

He stared at a picture of a space shark hanging above the bar

"And then the Plutonian says, 'I'll never have that part of my body removed again!' Get it you semi-hairless ape?" The Martian asked

Astro Al stared into his empty glass and said nothing

"Well it was funnier than your shark joke. Come on, let's get out of here. I know where all the five-breasted Orion girls hang out." the Martian said as he fell off the barstool

And somewhere far away another shark was disheartened

Gregory Damien Grinnell

The Undead Lover

I squeeze you in my arms
an ichorous liquid bursts from your
mouth like pus from an infected wound
I slash your wrists open and splay your
foreign blood upon the pages
they are soiled with your traitorous
black blood
Even in death you mock me
still dead you betray me
still I want more
Rape me with your eyes
Rape me with your dead eyes
my skin is covered with hungry mouths
their saliva is my sweat
you fill me with fluids of desire
traitorous desire
I walk the night with you, yet dead you are
Burn, my skin burns, licked by the tongue of your
    flame
So hungry, so unpure
Is there an end to this madness?
such an insane sadness
All my thoughts to your death and your life
when my weak flesh screams for you I can't fight
so I cry out to you and you laugh
as the smell of sickly sweet rot flows from your flesh
Welcoming me
Welcoming me into your embrace
A blissful sleep with eternal desire

T.G. Yearwood

Icon

I'm your king
I'm the hero of the hour
and I've got more than flower power
buy my CD, EP, LP, my book, my fashionable look, crawl
my web page, I want to be your sage, buy my CD-ROM,
watch my sitcom, wear my shirt, buy into my hurt, wear me
on your cap, let me hear you clap
I'd like to give you something new
let me ask my writers,
"Hey! Can you write me some new clichés? I'm sick of the
old ones."
Hey, remember those fifteen minutes Warhol told us about?
They're not going to be over for me, I won't suffer from
media fade-out
See, I've got bad attitude like John Shaft
and my charm is like witchcraft
My cool is like John Travolta
and my mind is like Minolta
It may be a stretch, but see
it all started for me
not when I saw Bruce Lee
but when I saw Electra Woman and Dyna Girl on TV
I knew I wanted the fame thing
so I could be somebody's nighttime plaything

David Stickney

Gregory Damien Grinnell

The fact that Elvis died on the same date that Madonna was born
isn't a coincidence.

The King just accidentally dying on that strumpet's birthday ...

I think not!

You know they can push their thoughts through the TV

Mayor Menino

says so

And EP wouldn't have liked MTV

They needed someone who did

so they got rid of him, bet they plotted it in the shadow of a
pyramid

And that means that those UFOs are in on it

and if I didn't think that the flying saucers were in on it I would be
a hypocrite

But the King knew

Oh yeah baby he knew

They tell me that they don't but I know they

talk about me behind the King's back

behind my back

the CIA, FBI, IRS, CID, CCD, GED, LSD,

IMF, and the WWF all said the same thing

They say milk has a half life

but I bought whole milk

Elvis drank buttermilk

It's all a big circle closing in around me

Just like being in a flying saucer

forced to read Chaucer

Like a virgin? As though I'm supposed to believe that!

It's all tied up with that Arafat, all those plutocrats, technocrats,

Foghat, and that no good deceitful Top Cat!
But me and the King know better
They got him
but not me
They won't get me
got rid of the phone
I live alone
keep my fluids safe
that was the King's only mistake
he didn't watch his intake
or his outtake

Derelict

A witch cries
out to God
as the dire
smoke from
her meat
ascends

Throw another
piece of wood
onto the holocaust
As she screams
higher
don't let your
humanity in

A little boy
living down
the drain
singing prayers
for dead rats
because they're
his only friends

Somewhere
someone
shakes her
head in mock
pity

and says,
"This is the
price they pay
for sin."

Didn't know
you could be so broken
let your sight slip
and become so vagrant
and all those aspirations
now so wooden and token

Couldn't realize
that fault spread
from so many places
and blame
is as plentiful
as cracks in the pavement

Slain by slander
starved by want
all that is done is merely profit
from their misery
And their memories
fail to even haunt

Witches are burned
crucified rodents
Vermin execution
offers only animalism

pleasures

at the sight of

punishment

for their heresy

Let them long for

strangulation

as another friend

turns enemy

A little girl

lives in a

wet pipe

a bag of

glue over

her mouth

it's the only

thing that

keeps the wolf

in her stomach

down

Little girl

glass of eye

phosphor burnt

and innocent in one eye

hopes to have dinner

someday

A uniformed man

offers chocolate and smiles

treats for orphans

A bullet for her skull
A bullet all her own
Better for her to die
than grow up derelict

T.G. Yearwood

A Blade of Grass

Where can
we hold
onto
on a speck
of dust
moving
over black ripples

Dance
she does
over grass
like oceans
sun washes
down
indifferent and
unknowing

She plucks
a blade
from the field
"Where am I?"
words drift in
from eclipsed valleys

In a forgotten
hallway in a
malignant city
Kitty Genovese

lies bleeding
with hollows
in her sockets

Move back
and architects
encompass
encapsulate
align
and
define

Dance
she will
her summer
fabric edge
touching the
tips of the
emerald-hued
blades

Never having
seen again
Never having
known again
two weeks
gone by
another friend
prone does lie

Designers build
on creation
but never do
they make

Random fall
patterns choose
but make
no choice

Spin
spinning human top
awhirl in a
hurricane of weaves

Green stains on
her garment
green stains on
her bare ankles

Ignorance
bliss of the
television
drips
into our
arms

Empires
build
themselves

down

horrors

revert

outwards

and

inwards

A summons

forgotten

"Be home by ten,"

shuffled aside

Twirling

pristine motions

in the rippling

jade

her fingers

pluck a slender

blade of grass

her voice

in her

ears

"Here I am on this blade of grass."

David Stickney

Varney the Vampire and I

One Halloween Eve I
went to a mall
where I
had to rescue
my undead friend
Varney
Who got
his fangs caught
in the costume of some guy
dressed like
Barney
On the way
home he said,
"I'm sorry,
I never liked
purple."
"That's okay," I said,
"I just wish
you bit that
kid dressed
like Urkel."
It was okay
with me
See,
Varney and
I
go way back
I met him

while I
was standing
at a magazine
rack
When I told
him
I was
a hemophiliac
he jumped
on me
like
a nymphomaniac
Later he told
me
he didn't like
hanging upside
down
with all those
vampire cliques
So I said
hey, let's
go get
some chicks
and he said
"I think that
this is the beginning
of a beautifully twisted
friendship."
and it
was

because

he's loads

of fun

Sure, he

can't lie

around

in the sun

but he's

no simpleton

he's quick

with

a pun

and not

hurt by

a gun

and he

does a great

impression

of

Charlton Heston

and

he gets me a

discount on

dental floss

as long

as I remember

not to wear

a cross

Gregory Damien Grinnell

Road
Gods

AN EPIC POEM

OF SEX

MURDER

AND

TWENTY-SOMETHINGS

David Stickney

all images in *Road Gods* by Gregory Damien Grinnell

"Sex is a power of the ancient mystics" Rain's words floated somber and cloud like from her mouth

Paul never had the chance to brandish a response for then the cafe door opened and all eyes went south

A female strode through the door with hair like ghost's blood red pale beyond surrender and dead love

Her Emerald Isle eyes swooped through the cafe and rested like hungry green falcons on the stool next to Rain

The newcomer sat upon the stool as though all her movements were arcane rituals and the stool was a lover she was rousing to newfound life

The air in the cafe hung expectant like an empty stage watched by an audience of famished jackals

The waitress ambled over to the new arrival

"A Coke and some fries if they don't taste of nothing but grease" she said and when she spoke it was all the sounds of Irish storms and the struggles on forgotten chartreuse shrouded cliffs where clansmen died before the Christian god chose to wear thorns upon his brow

The waitress meandered off A gnarled patron shifted and let his bulk settle then released a cough The eyes of the spectators settled back into their staid routines Observing the dirt on the floor tiles Scouting for flies in the skin covered soup

Rain's eyes flicked to Paul then back to the newcomer who seemed to have temporarily sapped power from the group

Paul tried not to let his eyes soak deeply on the vermilion tressed stranger Instead he looked at Rain and studied the sardonic smile that always hung on her face like a comedic masque

It drew him into its silent cacophony of laughter as it always had and forever would Even in long years away in the aged distance he would come to he would still find that smile in the attic box of his memories

"Traveling?" It was a question directed at Rain by the newcomer

"Yes Fortunately we don't live around here" Rain answered Her sardonic smile faced the fey face of the woman

"My name's Sinead"

"This is Paul My name's Rain"

"What are you doing out here?" Paul injected

"Traveling"

"Are you two married or dating?" Sinead asked

"Both Neither Whichever we feel like at the time" Rain replied

"Good I like things clear-cut"

They shared their first laugh together

It didn't stink of demons or scorched earth or the open naked limbs of hell

Nor was it open and bare empty caved in and denuded like an open shell

It was a shared laugh and nothing more

Sinead tasted one of the fries before her

"Miserable Limp Nothing worse than limp fries"

"Can't stand them either" she said between her sardonically framed lips

"Hate them" Paul added

"You need to use some ketchup on them anyways" Paul offered

"Drowning's too good for them" Sinead answered

Her forest like eyes looked into the blue/grey quiet of Paul's

A raven alighted from a telephone wire Somewhere there was night and a shooting star tasted earth

Portents and poetry

"Who are you and who were you then?" Sinead asked the lovers

"There's a familiar ring to that" Paul said

"Movie quote I think Still that's no answer to the question"

"We come from Boston Drove out in the 'It-Mobile'" Rain answered

"It-Mobile?"

"Our car All cars should be named The name gives them personality and spirit like ships They can never really die that way" Paul answered

"We left Boston to find something but we haven't found whatever it is that we we're looking for yet All we've really found so far is commercials and junk" Rain spoke her eyes peeling back mile by mile to the unanswered now that she sat in

"We were bored" Paul said as he too relived the past A job regular hours steady paychecks bills parents social ills dust corrosive rust apartments departments and no relief and no adventure color blind in a gridded mapped out rat's life

"We're like explorers I guess Sailors looking for new land" Rain said

"I prefer to be a goddess"

"How does one achieve that and what are the benefits?" questioned Paul

"A deity makes their own universe"

"What's your universe like?"

"It's hot and lined with the dead and soon to be dead"

"Doesn't sound like you have a great benefits package there" Rain replied

"I think it all depends on who's dead and who's soon to be that way" Sinead severed a fry with her yellowish teeth

"Now just how does one create a universe?" Paul queried

"You envision it Form it in your head Filter out all the crap in there The infomercials All the stuff all the crap they make us think is important Once you see it in your head you let the borders slip out onto the world Onto whatever world you're on at the time"

Paul laughed Metaphysics with a stranger in a cafe in the middle of a desert nowhere

It was too much

And yet not enough

There had to be more He wanted to hear more of her

Rain was impressed too

It was so much

And yet less than enough

Rain was touched by the earnestness of it The mythology and depth of it The psychology and death of it

Rain's straw sought out the last of the soda droplets in her plastic glass

"So what's the name of your creation?" Paul ventured

"It has no name If I were to give it a name it would limit it Refine it and somehow put it on a map so others, undeserving souls, could find it No it will never be named"

"How much do you charge visitors?" Rain questioned

"You just can't visit You're consigned there for the duration"

"The duration?"

"Forever"

"So what's the cover charge?" Rain asked, rephrasing her question

"Whatever I feel like charging Drinks are on the house"

"And what would our admittance run us?"

"A ride would be payment enough"

"If you don't have your own car how'd you get here?"

"Hitched a ride with a trucker"

"Pretty dangerous these days It's not the friendly Sixties anymore and the road isn't so kind now that the Dead Heads aren't all over it" said Paul

"It wasn't a big deal He wanted to fuck me"

The waitress drew her face up into a shrew like mask as she heard Sinead's last sentence

"So what'd you do?" Rain asked

"I let him in my universe"

At first that seemed answer enough

But Paul had to ask something

"What was his ticket price?"

"His life"

Sinead laughed

It was a friendly sound and it drew Paul and Rain in

"Excuse me Sinead while I confer with my girl"

Paul and Rain got up and walked a few paces away from
Sinead There was a small magazine rack in the diner They stared
at the periodical deforestations while Paul conferred with his girl

"Well do we give her a lift?" Paul asked in a secretive voice
saved for lover's conversations

"At least until we get to the next city It should be fun She
smells like adventure" Rain answered in a secretive voice saved for
lover's machinations

"Funny I thought she smelled of CK"

"Captain Comedian doesn't strike again" Rain answered after
a minute's pause

They returned to their seats

"Madame"

"Mademoiselle" Sinead corrected

"All right Goddess Mademoiselle you are to have the singular
honor of cruising along with us in the It-Mobile as we traverse to
our next destination" Paul said

"Ready"

"Don't want to finish those fries?"

"They were finished before I got them"

They counted out soiled bills and planted them on the
counter Sinead threw a crisp five dollar bill down on the counter

"Being a goddess pays well" she explained

They walked out into the desert heat and lusting spiral
sunlight They walked to a car that was not just a car

The red of cherries A white that should have been milk pure
but was just dust stained instead Fins that cut like sharks Too
titanic and lethal for dolphins Dust wall tires Silvery antenna
Toothy and predatory grillwork Convertible seduction

A 1958 Plymouth Fury

"Now I get the name" Sinead said with the Celtic sway of her
tongue

"Yeah I had it since high school Only car I'll ever own
Everyone wanted it Even got into a few fights over it" Paul's pride
caused him to speak in venerable tones

"Hence the name" Rain said as she ran a finger along the hood

"Any rough fights?" Sinead inquired

"Yeah one got a little bloody" Paul didn't elaborate

They piled into the car Sinead with her duffel bag and backpack Rain with Paul

Paul at the wheel

Open desert miles running past their windows

"It's all up and down this desert highway"

"What is?"

"My universe It lords over the road here"

Quiet a moment

"Do you want to be like that?"

"Lording over the road you mean?"

"Yeah do you want to be deities, demigods, demons, angels, messiahs, gods? Masters of the motorway"

"If it means free drinks I'm in" Paul answered

"If it means I get to live in a land that's never boring and isn't ruled by celebrity cults I'm in too" Rain said after a brief intermission for thought

They drove and spoke and the day was swallowed by night Shimmering road djinns whirled away under the surfaces of night

Rain said, "Motel ahead do we pull in for some sleep or what?"

"Yeah I could use some sleep" Paul said

They pulled into the motel parking lot

They parked and the car exhaled a silence which the trio sat in for a moment

"Are you two going to get a room or are you just planning on renting this parking space?" Sinead quipped

"We're um going to get a room If you want you can crash in the car I mean there's not much else around here" Paul offered

With that Rain and Paul departed from the car and went to rent a room

After they got their keys from a tired looking attendant Rain looked at Paul Then she asked, "Should we have, you know, invited her to crash with us in our room?"

"Do you think it's all right I mean giving her a ride is one thing but really we hardly know her"

"I think it will be OK"

"Are you sure?"

"Yeah"

They went to the It-Mobile and found Sinead sprawled out in the back seat divining for sleep

Rain knocked on the window and Sinead sat up and stared at the black haired girl so tidy under her blackened tresses

"Hey want to share a room with us?"

They entered the motel room so much like any other motel room Uniform design Spartan and barren of any feeling and teeming with insect life

Two chairs A table A cable-infused TV set A bathroom A floor One bed

Sinead looked at the pair

"Who gets the bed" she asked

"We do" Rain answered

"We all do?" Sinead asked

Rain's mind raced—should have seen this weirdo Paul was right what the hell was I thinking kind of exciting inviting is she kidding

"I can make you both gods this way"

"By jumping into bed with us?" Paul asked with incredulity smothering his words

"Yes Don't be so afraid We can build new mythologies tonight here and always"

Rain let the thought cascade and spiral down Her synapses firing away

"Let the old gods bleed with jealousy tonight The young gods with ancient powers can rule tonight"

Silence

"Well somebody decide If we're not going to have group sex I'm going to sleep" Paul said He knew his exhaustion would burn like a plundered city if the two of them were naked before him

Otherwise he wanted to see the inside of his eyelids

Rain put her hand on Paul's arm

Sinead approached them like a blood hungry angel Divine and evil

They joined

They knew the power of mystics both ancient and newborn

Lust centuries spilled beneath sheets rapidly stiffening fluid bath swirling hydras of sex screaming rain clouds shatter

the broken flowers

the old gods' flag is only a tatter

Morning

They arise like undead

Stiff and cold Hungry and feeling old

"What do they do for breakfast around here?"

"Don't know but breakfast is on the goddess" Sinead proclaimed

They traipsed into the dingy diner that served the motel

Rain wore sunglasses over the dark oceans of her eyes

Paul wore a tired upon his face that wasn't a mask

They strode in like crestfallen saviors and fell into a booth

Their only company was a middle aged man stinking of conservatism and his brow beaten wife

The man stared into them Envy and petty dislikes glowering on his face

They didn't care to notice

Over the ruins of their oily breakfast

Sinead lit a cigarette

She didn't smoke often but her mouth craved the taste this morning

"Hey look!" the man said to Sinead as he pointed at a no smoking sign faded and battered that hung over the counter forgotten and ignored by all but him

Sinead stared at the sign and then turned to the lone waitress The waitress shrugged her shoulders and offered a look of tired indifference

Paul read the trails of her dead life all over her face then he returned to looking at nothing

Sinead exhaled a vampiric gray cloud of smoke

"Put it out!" the man demanded

Sinead shook her head

She exhaled a cancer cloud and sipped some of the remnants of her coffee

He got up and walked over to them

"I said put it out!"

"No" Sinead said as it quietly burned towards her lips

"This is a no smoking restaurant!"

"First of all this is hardly a restaurant and secondly I think you're the only one who cares Besides we're sitting pretty far from you Why don't you just take it easy" Paul spoke as Rain stared at the man from behind the night world of her glasses

The man was not used to being defied It was all over his soulless face

He lashed back It was all he understood

"Put it out right now you little bitch!"

"Watch your mouth in the presence of ladies" Paul said

"What the hell are you going to do about it?"

"Hey why don't you both just calm down We don't want any trouble" the waitress said Even in her detached state she felt the onrush of storm clouds

"Yeah just lighten up Joe Suburbia" Paul said in the face of the tension

"Earl" the woman pleaded like a broken slave

Earl felt an emanation from the three Something edgy which frightened him He slowly went back to his seat but before he did he said, "Fucking punks I should kick your asses"

Earl threw down the money for his bill and left His wife in tow

Before she departed she looked at the trio and hissed, "Sinners"

"He felt it" Sinead said

"Felt what?"

"We're a pantheon now" Sinead said as she ground the corpse of her cigarette out

Out on the road four people were traveling in a car

An apocalypse was coming in with them

In the trunk of their car a dead body thumped in time with the movements of the vehicle

"For a fucking corpse he makes a lot of noise" one of them said as he lit his crack pipe

"Language" said the driver as he fingered the gold crucifix around his neck

They called him the Pope He was a minister of the Universal Life Church A sect which believes that anyone should be allowed to be a priest

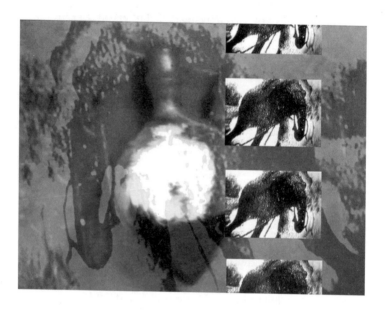

The one smoking crack used his real name Nadar Sarkisian His eyes held a permanent glaze He was bound in black leather clothes His father was from the Middle East

The one riding shotgun held a shotgun under his trench coat His name was Nate Mayer He worshipped Pope as though he was the truth and heaven sent

The girl in the backseat was called Easy because she was Her hair dyed green Her nails painted black One eye gray and calm The other pale brown and malevolent

"He must be pretty ripe by now" Nadar said as he passed the pipe to Easy

"Yes we'll need to stop and get some air fresheners to place in the trunk We don't need the police catching a whiff of our departed friend do we?" Pope said as his eyes scouted the highway

Hunting prey

"I'm still not cool with it Pope I mean it seems almost disrespectful to drag Pete's body along and it's risking cop trouble Heck even you admitted that" Nadar knew better than to swear again Once warned twice scorned

"Don't question his word" Nate said Reverence and awe

"Relax Nate, Nadar's concerns are legitimate Nadar, it would be disrespectful to Peter if he was not with us when we avenged him His remains should be with us when our righteous vendetta is handed out and the police won't be concerned with us as long as we take the proper precautions" Pope stated

"I guess" said Nadar

"What are we going to do when we get her Pope? I mean how are we going to hurt her?" Easy asked

Demons glistened Bright blood rose up

Hunger for the pain

"Her damnation shall be sacred Her sight has offended us So we shall remove each of her eyes Her hands have been used against us So they too will have to be lopped off Her feet must also be severed of course She must be kept alive to feel all of this She must be made aware of what blasphemes she committed against us" Pope said

Hunger of the insane

Easy smiled, "It'll be beautiful"

Pope smiled back at her through the rear view mirror "Oh yes A carnival of dusky æsthetics upon our sacrificial altar"

"The heretic must die" Nate said with the urge to crucify

They rode on

The corpse rotted on

"We can go any way we want" Sinead said

"'King of the highway', Morrison said" spoke Paul

"The Doors aren't bad" Rain stated

"I used to like them a lot until the guy who lived upstairs from me played them day and night And sang along, totally off key of course" Paul related

"Didn't he say something about starting a religion in one of his songs?" Rain asked

"Yes and planning murders" Sinead said

Rain turned and looked at Sinead

"An old boyfriend had some of their albums" Sinead explained

Rain stared at Sinead through the smoke world of her shades

"Hey, there's Joe Suburbia, Big Earl!" Paul said and pointed to the side of the road

"Trouble with the 'Salvation Station Wagon' it looks like" Rain said

As they drove by they saw Earl cursing the exposed engine of the car as his wife stood by rapt Shaded by the open hood

"Let's give him a hand" Paul said

"Are you serious?" Sinead asked

"Yeah why not? It would suck to break down out here I couldn't even leave a jerk like that out here"

"Yeah let's give him a chance to be civil" Rain said

They pulled the It-Mobile over and backed it up to Earl's ailing car

"What do you want?" Earl asked Face teeming with tension

"Saw you broken down and we just figured you needed a hand" Paul explained

"No We're fine" Earl sneered

"We don't want help from sinners like you" the wife hissed

"Hey lighten up Just thought you might need a hand but you don't so we'll be on our way" Paul said

"Don't talk to my wife like that you snot" Earl raged as if he actually noticed anything directed towards his wife

"What the fuck is wrong with you? I pull over to give you a hand and we get this? You're a dick Come on let's go" Paul said

"I've had enough of this shit too" Rain said

"What did you call me you little piece of You're going to get the ass kicking I promised you!" Earl said as he moved towards them Paul had been in fights He didn't feel he was an action hero or a weakling zero

But he knew he wasn't much against a man with a tire iron in his hand

Sinead handed him a pistol

He fired before thought shook his will He had fired pistols before A brother who was a gun buff

Earl twisted in the keen of the desert wind

Red spread on his shirt

Fell into the dirt like a tired top

Urine pool next to the blood twitch of a leg and all done

Sinead handed Rain a pistol and pulled another out for herself from her duffel bag arsenal

The wife stared at the shell that was Earl

Paul stared too Frigid motion in slow time

"One of us has got to do it" Sinead said to Rain, her pistol towards the wife

Rain knew Paul's brother

The bullet opened a tear in the center of the woman's face

She fell like dropping down from space

Rain lowered her smoking pistol

Sinead saw a flicker of movement in the car

She fired twice

A third time to make sure she hit

Glass clouds burst open into the dry air

They walked forward to see who she hit

A small boy on the backseat

His brains on the rear window

His blood splashed all over the car

"No" Sinead whimpered all the energy falling out of her

"Let's go Come on"

Paul grabbed Sinead's wrist and pulled her into the It-Mobile

Rain took the wheel and the It-Mobile threw dust into the air

Pebbles cast back Stoning the corpses

"Fuck"

"That guy would have killed me and probably raped both of you in front of his wife"

"They didn't bring their kid in the diner with them What did they do just leave him in the car?"

"There's no way they can catch us"

"Tire tracks"

"Wind will get rid of them"

"Waitress will remember us"

"Maybe but that's not proof"

"We can ditch the guns They'll never find them if we bury them out here someplace"

"Can't do that I need to sell them Besides we might still need them"

"Where did you get them?"

Quiet

"Did you ever kill someone before?" Rain asked Sinead

A moment

Then: "Yes The guy I got the guns from He deserved it Not like that kid No fucking way"

"What the hell? Did they just keep that kid locked up back there all the time?"

"Sinead I know we've just been through the wall here but what the hell went on with you? What do you mean you killed the guy you got the guns from? Did you really kill that guy who gave you a lift too?" Paul asked his grip on the pistol tightening

"No I mean I was joking about the ride The trucker he did want to fuck me I didn't He dumped me at the diner and took off"

She slowed dynamic explosive pulses of her heart Finally speaking again after a moment of calm

"The guy I killed He was part of this gang I did some stuff for him Dropped off packages picked up stuff Nothing more than that One night he wanted too much from me He looked like my father when he came towards me I then I grabbed the gun from his belt and shot him I took the money that was lying around and some guns and ran That was about a week ago now I guess Yeah seven days"

"What kind of a gang?" Rain asked sweat raining down from her forehead

"What?"

"Is it a big gang like in the 'Warriors'? Or just a couple of people?"

"There's four of them All pretty sick They sell crack, guns, all sorts of shit"

"How'd you end up with them?" Paul's stomach unknotted and then knotted again

"It's not easy to get a job when you ran from your country because you're sick of sucking your father's dick" Sinead said, her eyes shed water lines

"He made you blow him?" Rain asked

"Held a knife to my head" she said as she moved a red lock from her temple Paul saw a thin scar there Flesh monument to sexual atrocities

Paul could say nothing to that He reached his hand to her and squeezed Sinead's trembling bird of a hand

"Sinead" Rain said

"Yes"

"I

can't

imagine

how

low

that

must

have

made

you burn

I'm sorry" Rain said Miles between her and Sinead Never been raped Almost once but not close next to that

"Thanks It was like opening up a bright box of lies Everything I knew before that day was wrong" Slow and mournfully spoken

Quiet again and road noise

"It sucks to be Sinead" she said

"It sucks to be anyone" Paul said

"Not for gods" from sardonic lips

"I didn't have to kill him I mean I just should have scared the guy off That's all Waved the gun at him Why was he such a dick? I only wanted to help him"

"We had to have blood" Rain spoke another quick quiet broke"

What?" Paul stared at Rain The cryptic night of her hair The doll like features of her face What light was growing behind her eyes What light?

"To baptize ourselves We've bonded We killed what we have become, a family We're now a pantheon" Rain mused

"But I killed a kid What did he ever do Nothing He won't do anything now except rot What did I do?"

"You spared him a life of crap, junk mail, parents who locked him in a car in the desert heat Mercy" Rain intoned

The tiny monsters of silence cavorted in the car

Night curves fell and they found a motel in the middle of a dust bowl town

In the room they sat watching each other

"They think he's a messiah" Sinead said into the microbe crawling floating mauling regenerating air

"The gang's leader" Not a question Paul held the answer in his mind already

"He's called Pope He's some sort of mail order priest"

"Will they be after you?"

"Yes they must be looking for me Pope believes in revenge"

"We're going to need those guns How are we set for ammo?" Paul asked

"Plenty got a few more guns too I guess I don't need to sell them"

"How are you set for money? Rain and I have got about two grand on us"

"Twenty"

"Dollars?"

"Grand I took the money that was lying around when I killed Peter"

"Wow"

"We'll take care of them when they come Heap them up with the rest Bury them under the heels and wheels of the road gods" Rain sighed

"No more! I mean if we run into these guys and we have to we'll kill them but that's it I don't want any thrill killing or any crap like that We did what What happened back there happened but no more" Paul ranted into the cool distilled air

"We can be merciful" Rain suggested

Before any more words were offered Rain came to them

Feeding repleting cries of the dead arising ancient mansions of the dead hot storms of passion romance and sexual flicker taste so soon century of fragment spires of times agonies slick and saliva spent masticating reborn in the fetid sea smell of the motel room

They lay again in tiny operas of exhaustion

Overcome with the youth and eternal power of each other

"I think I love you both, but Rain you're beginning to scare me Tell me you're not going off You're still the girl who laughed when I told her the joke about the four guys on the plane" Paul said

"What's the joke?" Sinead asked Rapid gasps of air

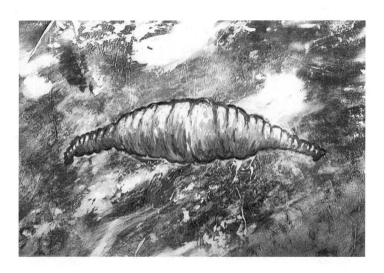

"There are four guys on a plane One English, one French, one American, and one Mexican"

Pope smiled at the waitress "That was delicious Tell me do you have any desserts?"

The waitress didn't smile back Mile upon mile of tolled years on her face

"The captain comes over the radio and says there's a fuel leak and if they're going to be able to make it they have to lighten the load So they start throwing all the chairs and junk out but the captain says they're still too heavy"

"Tell me, have you seen a rather striking young red head come through here recently?" Pope asked the waitress
She thought back
"Very Irish looking?" she asked
"Yes, she even has an accent that would make leprechauns envious" Pope said
"I think she came through here yesterday She was with another couple of kids I only remember 'em because they almost got into a fight with some guy"
"Please tell me anything you can remember" Pope implored

"So the English guy stands up and yells, 'God save the Queen!' and jumps out but the plane's still too heavy"

"Thank you You've been so very helpful" Pope said
There was only one customer besides them
A ragged trucker

"Then the French guy gets up and yells, 'Viva La France!' and he jumps out but the plane is still just a little over a hundred pounds too heavy"

"Here's your check" the waitress said as she placed the greasy bill face up in front of them

"In the quiet of the night do you know happiness?" Pope asked the waitress

Easy smiled

Nadar tensed

"What?"

"When the lights are extinguished for the day and your eyes draw closed are you happy or are you without love?" Pope asked

"I guess so" the waitress answered Bird retreating from a cobra's mesmerism

"So then the American guy yells, 'Remember the Alamo' and throws the Mexican out"

"I'm sorry No one should be pleased when the light fades We should all be hungry for so much more" Pope said

Nate stood as he drew his shotgun and fired it into the back of a trucker's head A cloud of gore smeared the booth

Nadar and Easy charged into the kitchen

Two more shots fired

Pope stood before the waitress with a pistol in her face

"I'm sorry you never truly knew the ravenous drives of life Don't cry I've already shed tears for you in my heart" Pope intoned

The muzzle flashed like fireworks

In death's empty repose she didn't look so aged at all

"That was stupid" Sinead laughed

Rain merely grinned and did not answer

Soon they fell into the arcs and the near distance sparks of sleep

In the morning they skipped breakfast

An infinite year upon year of far aways they wanted to lay between them and the slaughter they had wrought

Paul thought of asking Rain if gods feared the police

A tongue that wouldn't birth

They moved on No plans and nothing but escape sought

"Why does it have to hurt so much just being alive? All I ever really wanted was for the hurt to go away" Sinead said staring off from the passenger seat

"I thought that if I was above it all it wouldn't matter but you never get above the pain" Sinead said her throat swallowing only defeat

"You can change the pain warp it" Rain answered

"No more of this god crap" Paul moaned

"You can take the pain in The hurt is forever but if you change it, if you ride its currents and turn it back in on itself, you can turn it back on your enemies Make it your weapon Sinead Picture the gang, your father See them in your mind and one by one force the hurt to strip them down Shred them with your pain A deity can do this" Rain said

Sinead nodded

"Hey Celtic cutey" Paul called

Sinead turned and fixed him with an irreverent glare

"I always wanted to know, is it true they have no snakes in Ireland?" Paul asked

They all laughed

The music from the radio cut away to the news interplay

What they had waited for

Their crime

Police threats Random access violence and news of thrill kill sets

"Well our time has arrived the new theophany has been ushered in" Rain stated

"Do you think someone is working on a web page about us?" Paul asked

"Theo- what?" Sinead asked

They chased down disparate roads telephone poles ever the sentinels road signs like antiquated seers pointing the way internet information flowing along telephone veins overhead invisible information signals of communication streaming through them every multimedia word ever said

Easy slid into the backseat

"Was the attendant helpful?" Pope asked

Easy smiled "Yes, most He remembers three young people registering here one had red hair 'Like a sea of fire', he said They were driving one of those red cars like in that movie Christine"

"A '58 Fury That's a gem Could I have it Pope?" Nadar's eyes grew large with the bloating of want

"Certainly Nadar Easy, was he any good?" Pope stared into the rearview mirror reflecting eyes upon the woman

"His breath in my throat felt good but ultimately lost" Easy said recollecting grinding atop him (the attendant, name unknown) lips fusion melt

"Did you kill him?" Nadar asked wanting to leave no more dead in their choked wake than needed

"No He was weak He tasted of infestations He'll waste away on his own soon"

The night glared down at the It-Mobile
as it sailed over the ocean tides of roadway
All night they conspired to voyage
Sinead slumbered in the back
Rain's eyes moved across the desert plain crawling over every inch trying to keep track

"You never answered me the other night" Paul spoke eyes above the wheel

"About the joke?" her hand playful on his lap, grabbing a feel

"Uh yeah About you and the joke" trying to keep thoughts there and real

"Of course I'm not the same We're transmogrified We're no longer part of them" eyes casting dim twilight mirages upon him

"Who's them?" his coarse hand upon her hand smooth and slim

"People The consume or be consumed mortals The people who live off junk ideas and fast food catch phrases They're like walking piles of dust all around us" disdain the top down letting in the breath of night

"Because we killed that makes us better than them?" bitter venom sarcasm and blight

"No we were better than that before the killing because we saw through all the neon wallpaper bullshit but the killing made us even stronger We didn't cave in We didn't turn ourselves over to the cops We kept right on going and don't you feel the difference now?" desiring him to see

"I don't think so Fill me in" wanting now to see

"We're not looking for something anymore we've found it" at peace

He thought about this She was right No roaming searching meandering in himself anymore All was a now that he felt A triumvirate All the lost ways they had searched led to the slumbering friend in the backseat and the killing It was wrong he knew but perhaps it had its place A legend is not forged without nightmares

"Maybe Maybe you're right" not able to let the questioning cease

"I am The answers for us don't come without price tags"

"I'm going to pull over at that gas station We need to put some dinosaur bones into the It-Mobile's stomach"

They pulled into the lone outpost of human souls Pale pools of human light

Paul gassed the car

Rain went in hunting for caffeine

Sinead woke and went hunting for a bathroom

Paul moved the It-Mobile out of the light and parked it in the dark away from unwanted searchlights of eyes

He waited near the bathroom

A car turned into the station

Lights flowing across his retinas

Four people exited the car limbs stretching Leather creaking

Sinead came out of the bathroom

Hell laughed

Sinead felt the buffet of internal shock

Nate saw her before his companions did

His shotgun was pulled free from his coat

He pulled the trigger

It jammed "Heretic!"

Sinead pulled a gun

Easy dropped behind the car and pulled a gun

Nadar drew a pistol and fired, the shot roaring wide and afar
like dragons lost in the hot night
Pope dropped behind the car and drew two pistols
Sinead fired wild
Bullets slicing hot metal through the air Sparks off the car
Inside the station Rain dropped down She still had her gun
The attendant hit a switch calling the police and ducked
He arose with a gun and loosed its fire through the window
Glass pluming out

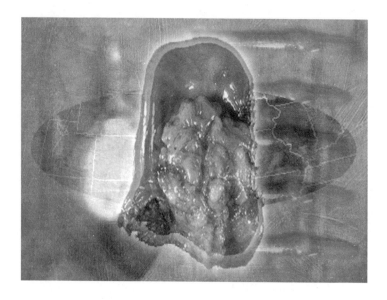

A bullet tore at Nadar's arm
He fired towards the station wild with hate wild with wild
Paul pulled Sinead towards the It-Mobile and cover
She fired again and again
Easy stood and fired into the station four bullets burst into the
attendant he fell to the floor twitching Rain looked at him
His shirt had the name 'Chip' sewn on it
Who named their kid 'Chip'?
They were out there

Rain stood and fired into the enemy

Nate couldn't clear his shotgun

Pope fired dual guns at the running pair, pushing boiling air past them They dove into the shelter of the It-Mobile

Rain fired her last two bullets

The first caused Nadar to look down

A red circle was in his chest

The second hit him in the stomach

He fell and left the world

"Fuckers!" Easy emptied her gun of bullets all of them flying into the gas station

Rain ducked Ring Dings cigarettes lighters matches soda cans jumped leaped pumped cavorted slumped distorted and screamed at the bullet's commands

Paul started the It-Mobile and spun it towards the station

Sinead leaned out the window and fired Nate dove over the top of the car leaving the malfunctioning gun in the dust Pope rose and fired into the office emptying both guns

Easy reloaded as the It-Mobile stopped in front of the door Rain jumped into the backseat

Paul fed fresh gas into the engine Gravel exploding behind them

Sinead fired twice more then the trigger clicked uselessly

Sparks

Pope screamed, "Into the car!"

He started it Engine roaring into life Easy jumping in Nate just clinging to the side of the hood

The car moved as smoke rose from near the pumps The It-Mobile already speeding ahead and away lights off Sinead and Rain reloading

"Can't believe"

"It was them"

"One of them is dead I think"

"They killed a guy who was working there He shot at them first"

"Is it on fire?"

"He called the cops"

"They'll know it was the same guns"

Orange and red lights blossomed behind them Rolling balls of red black and pure heat mushrooming up from the ground

"Thank God I had to piss" Sinead said

"You're welcome" Rain breathed

"Are they still behind us? I can't see them anymore" Paul asked

"If they are I don't see them Whatever you do don't take the first exit take the second"

"Okay"

A second exit came quickly and they took it hearing a siren not too close by

Paul ignited the lights

"Can't believe we lost them so easy" Paul said

"Lucky"

"What?"

"We have to be lucky sometimes" Sinead said as she finished loading the gun

"There was a power in the air A snap It was all so surreal and quick It was almost like a John Woo picture only it was real" Rain said as she finished loading her weapon

"But no one was wearing sunglasses" Paul quipped

No response

"Maybe we should get a room If we stay off the road for a while they might lose us" Sinead said

Hours sinking into the loss of the past

Night signs in a small off ramp town as the sun spills its hemorrhage of morning light

A motel found Rain found a spider under the bed Paul dubbed it their mascot Sinead threw it out the door

Rain went to the shower

Paul looked through Sinead's arsenal

"I guess I should keep one on me"

"It would be a good idea Next time if you're alone they'll" trailing off to where vermin feed carrion carousel

"What are they like?"

"Mad Pope claims they are his holy servants He just radiates a craziness He says Easy is their virgin whore I don't know"

"Did you pick up your god stuff from him?"

"Don't know Maybe Maybe I believed it before we killed them But Rain has taken it in"

"Yeah"

"I can leave I mean they may not have gotten a good look at you two I can buy your car and let them come for me"

"No" a final closing

Lighter flame touched to a cancer nail Smoke wafting over painted lips

"My father would never say anything about it"

"No"

"He would just look at me when he wanted me to do it Stare right through me His eyes felt like swollen bugs all over my skin"

Paul swallowed her in his embrace

"I can be what Rain wants me to be but only if we all live through this" Paul said Sinead melting into his chest

Rain came out of the bathroom towel draped Wetly dripping

"Seems you're both ready"

Towel falling drawn gravity pulling

diaphanous droplets of water sparkling tiny pinwheels of light electric torment rippling flesh waves tongues of domination kissing caressing undressing her sinful sensations soft mute screaming neck thrusting nails tearing shearing down exposed lowlands of skin dawn carnivore caresses so deflowered lips denuded consummate unbroken necromancy invocation bestial stimulation rendered asunder sybaritic suckling open channels of wet shores microscopic murders vibrant anthropomorphic dryads and celestial titans

All finding closure in touching

"I don't know if I can take another night of this" words scrabbling up Paul's bleached throat

"Wimp" Rain said as she fell into a secret limbo behind her eyelids

"Listen" Sinead whispered from her soiled mouth

The sounds of a tender rainfall tapped against their motel room

Paul smiled and tasted the parasitic hunger of sleep

Sinead listened to the declining and reclining of their sleeping drones

She slumbered then and any agony that her father caused her was cleansed by the rain

"I'm sorry Pope My gun just wouldn't work" Nate said He was kneeling before Pope

The side of some road Cactus witness Engine running Lights circling out into the night

Easy squatting behind them Trickle of fluids

"There is no need of this" Pope said

"But I must be punished" Nate cried He ripped his shirt from himself and drew forth a powerful flayed whip

He began to lash his own back Welter his own flesh with the leather curse of the whip

Easy strode to the pair

"I wish we could have brought Nadar with us He could have kept Peter company in the trunk" Easy said as she leaned against Pope

"Yes poor Nadar will never know the release beloved Peter will" Pope said as he watched Nate injure himself Back all bleeding and mauled

"Enough Nate Arise you are of no use to the quest if you need to be taken to a hospital I give you a new weapon" Pope handed Nate an Uzi machine gun

"Take this and know my blessing"

Nate smiled as salt tears stabbed his eyes

Beneath their feet

under the dirt

in unlit tunnels

ants waged war

The It-Mobile rolled too impatient to stay still for long Driving by vagaries and gas stations

Towns motored by Nameless faceless squalid in the dirt
like the towns on toy railroad sets fake balsa wood hollow
lifeless

"My stomach gauge is on empty" Paul proclaimed fingers
tapping the wheel

"Oh stop it All we do is eat, fuck, and drive" Rain said as she
leaned over and nipped Paul's ear

"Like that's such a bad thing"

"This is coming from Mr. I Can't Take Much More Of This"

"That was hours ago"

"Let's do something different tonight Let's go to a club and
drink" Rain pleaded

"We're going to go get bombed while a gang of lunatics is
looking for us? That idea doesn't even rate on the scale of bad
ideas That idea is on a whole new chart of stupidity"

"We're going anyways"

"Why? And you know you haven't even asked Sinead"

"As long as we go armed I don't care If they're going to find us again does it matter where we go?" Sinead asked "What kind of clubs are we going to find out here? I don't want to go to some country and western mother dating bar"

Rain laughed, "We'll find something I don't want to go to some cousin kissing, sheep loving, grits eating, dating your brother who's also your uncle, line prancing, buck toothed, Trisha Yearwood is my cousin and my wife bar"

"Well said"

diffusion of day into twilight

As the moon rose and bloomed in the sky they found a place

A club

washed in lunar light

The Illusion Club

Simple and ominous in its blackness

parked on a side street

through the door armed each one of them

A small cover charge

Then they are in

exploding strobe dreams of colour

Techno industrial trance hypnotic pulses of music driving from speakers in one room

Another is quiet Music only spilling in from elsewhere A smaller bar and a pool table Darts are tossed

The other room is small A live lounge act performs all pseudo hipness and pretend cheese

"Good choice" Paul said

Rain merges with the writhing convulsing group upon the techno saturated dance floor crowd Fog and cigarette smoke mingle Lights drive stab and pulsate

Paul looks for a menu if there is one

Sinead drinks She looks at her companions She never meant for her life to overlap and drag theirs down She could leave now Both occupied leave them some money and be away no more problems for them but she knows she could not leave its selfish but she can't She loves them It's a selfish reason to stay but it's the only one she has

Paul finds there is no menu

Rain dances oblivious to the circling desire of eyes around her She dances remembering meeting Paul at a party so many eons ago laughter a few dances and then she knew there was no more wanting She hadn't felt like she had needed something again until they had hit the road He had held her still for so long and she was glad Now the racing within her had stopped again and she was glad she knew where she was

She knew she was in her universe and so were they

Paul looks about himself

If he drew his gun and fired randomly would Rain be horrified? He knew that Sinead would be But would Rain be? Would she write it off as the power of the gods? The privilege of the gods? No she would be mad She couldn't have turned around so much become so bad

He placated himself with that and drank a beer one of seven he would drink upon that night Sluggish the next morning groggy to be sure but not hung over Miraculous almost But not celestial enough

Rain left the dance floor as Sinead entered

Rain drifted to Paul sweated pulsed gratified sanctified

His fourth beer Well on the kaleidoscopic transcendent drunken climb

"Do you remember a story you told me about when you were a little girl?"

The sardonic smile looked back at him

"It was the first Fourth of July you remembered Your father had roman candles He fired them and when they lit up you thought they were as big as the world and maybe those colors that came out could make the world and maybe the world could be as big and full of color as the fireworks" He drank more of his beer swimming in his vision unparalleled fields and plains

"Is the world that big now? Did the killing, the guns, fill the world with all the colors you wanted?"

"Have another drink The past is only behind us It's nothing else but dead time" Rain said eyes charting the confines of the club

"Paul, the world is full of so many more colors than that now

The light that I saw then is so dim, so much less than what I'm seeing now Let it go, isn't it enough that I love you and Sinead?" Stare intent and heavy with folklore

Paul didn't meet her look Stared off, watching the dancers, someone ordering a drink A woman playing at being a whore

"It can be if we don't let the world be ripped apart There has to be a way out I don't want to keep on like this forever I don't want to be staring into the shadows looking for this Pope guy"

"There doesn't have to be a way This may never end but we can face them and what they bring"

"What's that?"

"The future"

"Hey the both of you look too sedate Let's dance Let us gods revel and make merry" Sinead said as she shimmied towards the couple

Both joined her on the dance floor miming sex limbs trembling with intent gyrating forms and pulsing in synch with digital music beating bleating bleeding

Rain thought that now if she saw the balls of color shooting up into the blanket of sky, she knew she could shoot them Put bullets right through them Paul didn't understand but it didn't matter Tomorrow she could make him understand Tomorrow ever hurtling towards them would give her the time she needed to explain it to him

Death was what it is It didn't matter She could give life or end it She wasn't part of a young romany anymore She was no longer lost in the pop culture morass Her roots were everywhere and she was infinite and so were they

What else meant anything?

Nothing

They danced, writhed, and weaved in accentuated slow motions freeze frame vertebræ slamming collage of ambient flashes of lights They watched the lizards and wizards of lounge for a time Then breezed into the quiet room and stretched their domain to the pool table Then sunken in their wearied frames club lights up full they made their way to a motel like an ancient keep seemingly barren of life forms fell into a bed and soon were petrified by gelid galaxies of sleep

Closer to midday than morning they clambered into the It-Mobile and made their way out to the steepled and less peopled borderlands of the town

"You look pretty tuckered out hipster and we didn't even do the horizontal macarena last night what gives?" Rain asked from behind the wheel

"Food I need to sop up all the hops in my system with some tasties" Paul said looking out upon the landscape with Rain's sunglasses

"I'm a bit peckish myself" the red haired siren chimed in

"OK A food dispensary it is"

They pulled into a parking lot tiny pillars of dust toppling by their tires

The Mug and Ladle is the name

They enter the eatery like slutty seraphs and an alcohol bruised satyr

Rain wore a tight belly shirt Jeans like blue dye

Sinead a rumpled dress of black and shortness

Paul a faded T-shirt corporate emblem forgotten Jeans like faded blue dye

Led to seats towards the back Somehow they still exuded control to the mildly busy establishment

"That was a good find last night Kudos to Rain" Paul said raising an obsidian coffee Still partially drunk eyesight swinging like crazed camera angles

"Thanks"

"I didn't think that I'd have a good time but I was wrong who would have thought such a place existed in a dumpy town like this"

Paul saw two kids walk past them battered Power Ranger dolls in their hands One pink the other red Keyed a chain of thought

"Who was the first celebrity you had a crush on?" Paul asked anyone as he laid the sunglasses down

"Greg Brady Sure he wore goofy clothes and stuff but all the girls seemed to like him and it made me curious about him Plus he had a smile that could be innocent or dangerous Like the time he tried to pretend he was a jerk so that a girl who wanted him would go after Peter instead" Rain said feeling mildly embarrassed dreading a put-down

"Elvis You see TV's not as big there Or at least it wasn't while I was growing up But I remember seeing Elvis and seeing him wiggle his hips and hearing his voice It was so American I wanted in right then" Sinead said inner eyes tuned to the viewpoint of an untainted girl

"And you, Johnny Bravo, was it Marsha?" Rain asked embarrassment dispelled Finger in a lock of hair curl and uncurl

"Wonder Woman, Lynda Carter" Paul said eyes glazed in a memory haze

"What a shock" Rain mocked diverting his incoming daze

"When she used to spin to change into her costume Well I didn't know what to call what it made me feel like then, but I loved that feeling anyways Never missed an episode Neither did my dad I don't know if it was the uniform or how she fit in it but it was stunning"

"You know they were all icons once Gods Totems Now they're gone and our rule has begun Who will sing our praises when we're gone?" Sinead asked the air

"We won't be gone Some myths are eternal" Rain voice from distant spheres

With a jezebelian jiggle Easy walked in and tapped Pope on the shoulder

"Is there much of a wait?" she asked him

"No my precious we should be seated soon"

"Good I'm going to the bathroom"

"Again? You really do excrete far too much"

She smiled and began to make her way to the bathroom

Pope and Nate were seated and looked over their menus

"I'd like to kill the twit who invented TV commercials He ruined everything Our whole world turned into a giant advertisement after that" Paul complained

"It goes back further than that I mean what were traveling medicine shows but infomercials on wheels Snake oil for the masses" Rain spoke the ebb and flow of her breath carrying her words into them

The waitress placed their drinks on the table One slipped Sweating glass tumbling in air spinning over ice striking floor tiles Glass fragments race into corners frantically trying to disappear

Pope turns to the direction of the noise slowly slides a menu up obscuring part of his face Culinary camouflage

"Nate, go get Peter The enemy is among us"

No hesitation Nate is smoothly quietly like an intangible ethereal nothingness He is gone to the car to the trunk opens it like a casket lid heedless of the swampy corpulent cloistered stench he puts his hands on the corpse

"Peter waken We're at the end of the chase"

"You both complain about ads so much but I think they were created to weed out the idiots Besides you're a god Erase them from your world" Sinead said

"The problem with that is, there wouldn't be much left"

A woman's scream Ripping horror crumble an Earth away

A dementia orchestra of staccato voices all at once in fray

They saw

Nate stood in the swirl of panic a dead body in his arms all full of love

Sinead knew his face

Pope stood to unleash the beasts of his pistols

A man yelled, "You're under arrest!" as he flashed a gold badge at Nate

Pope turned upon him and sprayed metal death The man spun in a crimson fury of splashing fluids The glass around him began to detonate

Rain and Paul flee the booth seeking cover Sinead frozen in web wave shock time caught

A table top next to Pope erupts as a misplaced bullet strikes it Pope wheels and exchanges shots with the undercover's companion Ballistic onslaught Paul dives back into the booth and wrenches Sinead to the floor eyes grow clear as terror and real time hit mental pathways Rain crouches and fires at Pope A roaring shot that goes wide amidst the diving panicked mob fleeing the open holy war

Nate drops the carcass and pulls the Uzi free Too many between them and the blasphemers He squeezes the trigger An explosive swarm of bullets tear into witless patrons blood jets and food splatters

The bathroom door opens Easy is out gun drawn sexually rabid for the eavesdropped violence She doesn't squander time for thought she fires twice a waitress hits the floor spine dying slowly survive but not calling it that forever helpless chair bound spoon fed dignity destroyed

Paul joins in Fires shots at Easy who dives behind a booth dripping crimson gobs and whimpering wounded sobs

Sinead stands resolute in the jaws of the maelstrom riding the borders of madness and cultivated chaos she fires into the stark open Nate's throat gapes open blood fountains out He still fires

More customers bullet dance and topple twitching as they become mindless meat Another bullet hits him in the waist He feels urine running hotly down his leg He wants to ask Pope's forgiveness but his throat will not work He squeezes the trigger The gun no longer even aimed, its last bullets fragment windows Another shot tears the side of his face open exposing teeth, gums, muscles, tissues, blood, and visceral issues He falls begging Pope for forgiveness

Forgive forgive the sky burns away

Pope's arm stings as a bullet tears at it He jumps onto a table and gets the angle he needs The undercover is out of ammunition Pope empties a round into the man's head Red all gore and burning rivers oceans lakes and seascapes of viscous red Pope dives for shelter as a round from Rain's weapon cuts a thin cat scratch across his back He begins to reload

"Do you have many bullets left Sinead? I believe you'll find Easy and I are sufficiently armed" Pope shouted as he slid an ammunition clip into place

"You're going to die so bad bitch that your fucking grandmother is going to wish she flushed your mother!" Easy screamed as she stood and opened fire Behind her in the kitchen food burned unattended Boiling water overflowed machines witless and submitless cycled onwards

Glassware and cutlery showered salt and sugar blew snow clouds over tables A cowering customer was struck in the eye by a shard of glass He lives but can remember little of the carnage and is forever visionless in one eye He dies a frightened old man fear at the slightest snap of sound the only witness to the entirety of the battle

Paul fires thrice at Easy A napkin holder jumps off the counter behind her

Rain fires Easy fires Rain's arm is scraped by a slug A bullet rips into Easy's shoulder she's jerked back puppet like struck with a steel shrike Sinead fires a bullet shatters Easy's hip Rain empties her last rounds into Easy She falls sideways and jerks electrically pulsing neurons imitating life rapidly cooling body eyes gazing on pools the color of Sinead's hair then gazing at nothing A wax dummy's stare

Pope rises up malevolent tower of pure incarnate sentient gleam of malignant malefactors maleficence manifest

Rain is standing out in the open A florescent light flickers like heat lightning above her Her gun vacant of death bringers

Pope fires

Paul slams his body into Rain's waist knocking her to the ground Her head is laid bare One eye gone one ear red glitter fruit jellied matter sliding out of her open skull

No soliloquy Her mouth frozen not in a sardonic pose but in a fissure of pain

A black opened in Paul

Pope fires again wild spray of lead Rain's sunglasses jumped and landed webbed devastated fractured and fragmented A bland framed print of artwork falls like a guillotine hitting Sinead in the back Small glass shivers and slivers sink into her skin like pins guided by dæmonic claws Sinead shoots without aim Bullets winging wide out in free falling space cutting into no flesh formica powder clouds coffee mug eruptions

In the kitchen grease hot and heated splatters like blood

Sinead's gun is barren she looks at Paul helpless All remaining bullets living in the It-Mobile waiting like solemn guardians, avengers, killers, and slayers

Paul is not sure how many bullets he has left count lost in the dizzying speed fire of the armageddon

"Pope!"

"Yes?"

"Sinead tells me you think you're god"

"I do not think I'm god I am bearer of his holy word His angel of chaos I am only part of his will"

"Well guess what? I am a fucking god and I'm going to kill you and your god's fucking words It's time that your part of my will was re-written Fucker!"

"Watch your language sinner!"

Paul stood madness and ice cold sparkle in his veins in his

spine snap and crackle of open challenge knowing maybe there were no rounds in the gun none left in the gun

Paul stood were Rain had stood

Pope remained concealed

Paul fired heedless of emptying his gun

Burning red streaks through the room ricochets darting by Pope cutlery cavorting at the bullets' whims

In the kitchen linen and towels offer themselves up to the maw and warm dimensions of the fire expanding spreading smoking choking

Pope stands once more The boy's gun is empty as he is, delusions of godhood What pagan insanity All the world must be cleansed of his influence

Pope smiles into the face of his adversary

He raises both his pistols steady aim An immobile target

One gun clicks jammed or empty

The other expels lead

The projectile slams into the wall behind Paul

Paul pulls the trigger In his eyes and in his mind all he knows is that Rain is dead and gone Welters of hurt

Pope feels a pain in his chest

Paul's gun roars like all maelstroms and tempests ever wrought flowing down the barrel and out the muzzle and through the room and into Pope's punctured frame

Paul fires and fires until the gun is dryly clicking and he has forgotten his enemy's name

Pope's right arm spasms as lead bites into it

His lower jaw disintegrates in mists of tooth bone blood nerve particles His waist is wet with sticky fluids pouring out of himself Another scalding hole in his chest His eyes float smolder with unrest Can not expire before the heretic

He shoots another round

Then falls like a soiled sack of rotted meat

The bullet slices by Paul's arm slicing a thin streak of his tissue open He is not aware of it or its passing heat

Sinead stands and grabs him

"We have to go"

Flame fanning fingers spread sumptuous blaze of fire from out of the closed doors

They stagger out an exit

Unseen in the confusion hollering halos of police sirens ambulance fire roars of spinning lights

The It-Mobile comes alive and they drive slowly away into the late afternoon oblivion

Years later they will both return here The It-Mobile battered but somehow voluptuous and still running Both missing her beyond all hopes Their child will be with them blissful and sainted in her lack of knowing They will retrace their steps Finding everywhere they were and everything they were They will not find the Illusion Club People asked no one knowing of it Directions checked listings sought Nothing No remains No identity They wonder if it ever was and how many bullets the gun held How many she might have given them They miss her still, forever ever will Their daughter, Rain, smiles up to the veldt of blue perfect sky and waits for the pristine figure she sees in her dreams, the one with a smile so special, to come down to her

About the Artists and Photographers

An artist and photographer, David Ladd Stickney attended school at the Art Institute of Pittsburgh, Salisbury State College in Maryland, and the University of North Carolina. With an interest in graphic design, he has turned most of his attention to the engaging world of photography. Living a mild-mannered life as a marketing rep for a photo lab, he aspires to making a living with his photographs and artwork.

T.G. Yearwood is a 26 year old freelance illustrator, graphic designer, animator, comic book penciler, and photographer. He currently resides in the Tidewater area of Virginia. When asked why he came out of self-imposed exile to create four pictures for Paul Angelosanto's newest book he replied, "What other poet could take Poe's bird and leave Jim in the dust? I'm glad to be a part of the project."

Gregory Damien Grinnell has traveled the world playing a variety of instruments in a myriad of bands (including ska-kings The Toasters) and doing multi-media projections for the legendary industrial band Prong. After turning his back on a career in music for the greener (or redder, yellower, etc.) pastures of the art world, Greg moved to Boston. He enjoys creating images both with computers and using traditional methods. You can visit his web site at http://www.citydog.com or you can e-mail him your suspicions about flying saucers at groenendael@worldnet.att.net.

About the Author

Paul Angelosanto is a poet, writer, artist, and actor. Some of his writings have appeared in: *The Boston Globe, Instant Magazine,* and *The Sour Grapes Newsletter.* Paul is an aspiring alcoholic who someday hopes to marry a Playboy Playmate. Despite some people's claims, he has never been abducted by aliens.

Colophon

This book was designed by Steve Norton at Red
Notebook Creative Services, Medford MA.

The body text is set in Jan van Krimpen's Spectrum
(roman and italic), by Monotype.

The display titles are set in Chank Diesel's
Moonshine, from the Chankstore
(www.chank.com).

The photo captions are set in Hermann Zapf's
Zapf Humanist, by Bitstream.

The title to "Al's Adventures In Space" is set in
Chank Diesel's Couchlover '97. The dingbats are
from Bill's Dingbats by Bill Tchakirides.

The cats are from Michelle Dixon's Woodtype
Ornaments, from Dixie's Delights; the fleurons are
from Robert Slimbach's Minion Ornaments from
Adobe.